HOW CAN A WOMAN PRAY AND BE SURE GOD WILL ANSWER

HOW CAN A WOMAN PRAY AND BE SURE GOD WILL ANSWER

A PRAYING CHRISTIAN WOMAN

WILLODINE HOPKINS

authorHOUSE®

AuthorHouse™
1663 Liberty Drive
Bloomington, IN 47403
www.authorhouse.com
Phone: 1-800-839-8640

Published by AuthorHouse 10/08/2014

ISBN: 978-1-4969-3035-4 (sc)
ISBN: 978-1-4969-3064-4 (e)

KJV
Scripture quotations marked KJV are from the Holy Bible, King James Version (Authorized Version). First published in 1611. Quoted from the KJV Classic Reference Bible, Copyright © 1983 by The Zondervan Corporation.

Dedication

This book is dedicated to: Paula (Williams) Seay

Paula (Williams) Seay is the oldest child of your author, Willodine Hopkins. In 2012, Paula was stricken with a severe case of pneumonia. Almost immediately after being hospitalized, the infection went septic, causing her to become comatose. Just as immediately, Paula's family began praying for her. With Paula's husband having eleven siblings, each of these individuals quickly expanded the prayer process through their church families. Of course, Paula's mother and siblings were also praying and expanding their prayer process through their church families. In addition, contacts were made through friends and acquaintances across the United States and overseas via Facebook. After the first week of treatment, Paula's doctor cautioned her husband to be prepared for the worst. Then again, after the second week, the doctor restated his precautionary warning. Sustained by the power of prayer and encouragement from many friends and loved ones, the grace of God brought about recovery. Although, the process required three weeks of hospital treatment and eight weeks of rehabilitation for Paula's body, which had practically ceased to function, her vitality was restored to a level allowing her to return home. With continued outpatient treatments, personal care, and medications, Paula has regained most of her mobility – save her right foot, which remains numb and mostly unresponsive. Paula's state of well-being today is a direct result of the grace of God through the power of prayer.

FAITH – HOPE – LOVE

Table of Contents

Part I

Prayer Issues and Situations
In the Life of A Christian Woman

Part II

Alphabet for A Praying Christian Woman

Part I

PRAYER
ISSUES AND SITUATIONS
IN THE LIFE OF
A CHRISTIAN WOMAN

To be purposeful and effective, prayer:

1. Must be understood.
2. Must be consistent,
3. Must be honest.
4. Must be offered from a loving heart.

**God will listen to prayer;
We must also listen to God!**

Chapter 1

Purpose of Prayer

At first, looking at the title statement, one may say, "To talk to God, of course! That question is easy to answer!" But when one re-reads the Genesis account of creation and considers Adam talked to God from the sixth day of creation, one observes no Bible scholar has ever believed or written Adam prayed to God from the beginning. This narrative is considered 'dialogue with God', but not true prayer because the context of the Biblical account is not what we Christians today consider true prayer.

When we meditate seriously on how Adam and Eve lived together in the garden, we frail humans cannot imagine a sinless world. Adam and Eve actually lived in a beautiful sinless world, with only one *"Thou shalt not"* command from God. *"Thou shalt not eat from the tree of the knowledge of good and evil, for when you eat of it you will surely die* (Genesis 2:15)."

This command was given to Adam before all other animals and Eve were created. Your author believes he was given this privilege in order for him to become aware there was no suitable mate for him because when Adam observed male and female elephants, male and female horses, male and female kittens, et al... he came to an alarming awareness there was not any of God's new creatures suitable for him. God put Adam into a deep sleep and took one of his ribs and made woman. When Adam saw Eve, he joyfully considered her as God's created mate for him. It was love at first sight.

For this reason a man will leave his father and mother and be united to his wife, and they will become one flesh (Genesis 2:24). Consider the meaning of "one flesh." This expression is the Biblical way of saying "joined together intimately." Every woman remembers vividly her first sexual experience. After Eve experienced the meaning of 'One Flesh,' with Adam, she too, always remembered.

God told Eve *"I will greatly increase your pains in childbearing: with pain you will give birth to children. Your desire will be for your husband and he will rule over you."* Some ancient Bible historians say Eve had over fifty children.

It has been truly said, "If you do not believe that the Bible is the word of God, please give a non-Biblical reason as to why women suffer so intensely giving birth to a baby?" Non-Biblical scholars are puzzled as to why women suffer intense pain when she has a baby. Some Biblical scholars compare human childbirth to the spiritual new birth humans experience when they are born into the Kingdom of God:

1. A woman comes to the realization that she is a sinner before God and that Satan is ruling her life.
2. She begins to strive for a way to not live in this manner.
3. Because she is anxious to please God, she comes to an acute awareness of her sins.
4. Then she begins to study the Bible. As she studies the life of Jesus, she learns even the sins she considered 'little', if not forgiven will keep her out of heaven when she dies. The Bible says any 'sin is sin.' What an awesome thing to learn!
5. She was taught Jesus is the Son of God, and the only Savior from sin in this world. So she confesses to others she truly believes Jesus is the Son of God; then is baptized (immersed) in water (John 3:5-8).
6. These actions caused her to be a 'born again' Christian, and she learned the term 'Baby Christian' applies to her.

Becoming a Christian Woman

Giving up sin is painful. It is the most difficult part of God's plan for salvation. Questionable language, indecent clothing, cheating on our income taxes and not getting caught, or any behavior that makes us feel and/or act superior to any other human is sin. God commands all known sin in our lives must be repented of and stopped as nearly as we weak humans are able. Sincere repentance expresses itself in giving the sinner a deep agony of the realization of the heavy weight of sin to a human soul.

Confessing belief that Jesus is the Son of God is not easy for many women because they are not comfortable speaking before an audience. God commands a public confession of a person's belief that Jesus is truly the Son of God before he/she is baptized.

Baptism is not painful, but it is a humbling experience. When people see us getting wet in the waters of baptism, some are joyful; because it is inspirational to them. Others question the necessity of baptism and argue that baptism is not necessary. The Bible teaches that baptism is commanded in order to receive God's gift of salvation from the curse of our sins (Acts 2:38).

If you have been baptized into Christ, write three sentences telling of your baptism.

_____

_____

_____

_____

_____

_____

If you have never been baptized please consider: Baptism is an essential part of the new birth. Jesus said: *"I tell you the truth, no one can enter the kingdom of God unless he is born of water and the Spirit. Flesh gives birth to flesh, but the Spirit gives birth to spirit. You should not be surprised at my saying, 'You must be born again.' (John 3:5)"*

You are all sons of God through faith in Christ Jesus, for all of you who were baptized into Christ have clothed yourselves with Christ. There is neither Jew nor Greek, slave nor free, male nor female, for you are all one in Christ Jesus. If you belong to Christ, then you are Abraham's seed and heirs according to the promise (Galatians 3:26-29).

Many sincere believers are taught if a penitent sinner prays the "Sinner's Prayer," this is the new birth and he/she becomes a Christian. The Bible does not teach this. The Bible teaches if a person examines himself/herself and becomes aware he/she is indeed a sinner who is out of covenant relationship to God and desires to become a child of God (Christian):

1. He/she must truly repent of the sins in his/her life.
2. Believe and confess publicly he/she believes Jesus is truly the Son of God
3. Be baptized (immersed) in water. The water can be a running creek, a lake or a baptistery with water deep enough to be sure every bit of the body is covered completely with water.

Then he/she will rise up out of the water a new creature, a true Christian.

The Age of Accountability

Why does your author stress baptism so heavily when this book is about prayer? All persons who have reached an age where they recognize sin in their life have reached 'the age of accountability;' they are accountable to God for their sins. "Accountability" means they know what sin is, and they have committed sins. The Bible teaches the only way a person's sins can be forgiven is through being truly sorry for their sins and being baptized in the name of the Father, the Son, and the Holy Spirit. Sins are washed away at baptism. Baptism puts a person into Christ. If a person is in Christ, that person can pray in Jesus' name and God will listen to their prayers.

The New Testament teaches the first church (group of people who became followers of Jesus) was established on the Day of Pentecost after Jesus returned to heaven. Three-thousand persons were baptized that day because they wanted to be <u>saved</u> from the consequences of their sins (Acts 2:38).

Write a prayer thanking God for something He has done to bless you in your life. Use indelible ink and strong paper. Seal it and put instructions on the envelope that it is not to be opened until your death. This will be one of the greatest blessings you can give your family. Use strong paper and seal the envelope with good glue. The ink may fade somewhat and the paper turn yellow - expect that, but the powers that answered that prayer will never fade.

Meditation Questions

(Think before you answer)

1. What is your earliest remembrance of hearing someone pray?

2. Listening to someone else pray helps many to draw others closer to God, but some are not affected. Why is this so - there are no wrong answers?

3. Jesus prayed often when HE was here on earth. He performed so many great miracles; it seems that His prayers were not for power. Why do you think it was important to God and to HIM to pray often? What is the lesson for us?

Chapter 2

PRAYER: IN THE BEGINNING

It surprises many people to learn that the first prayers of God's new creation were not recorded in the Bible. However, God walked and *talked* with Adam and Eve. Prayer, real prayer, is considerably more than merely conversation with God. This is not to demean the conversations Adam and Eve had with God, but simply to point out those conversations were NOT prayer as God commands Christians to pray today.

*Adam lay with his wife again and she gave birth to a son and named him Seth, saying "God has granted me another child in place of Abel. **At that time men began to call upon the name of the Lord** (Genesis 4:25B).*

Before sin entered the world, all creation was perfect and beautiful beyond our imagination to describe. Our finite minds have trouble merely trying to imagine a perfect world. No house flies, no blood-sucking- disease-causing mosquitoes and no headaches, no fever, and no tired aching back muscles sore from hard labor. Flowers bloomed in abundance and could be enjoyed constantly and never needed weeds removed because there were no weeds. It is believed that the weather was perfect. No icy cold mornings or no sweltering tropical heat to cause discomfort. Splendid sunrise greeted each day and stunning sunsets and starry skies gave beauty and glory to every night.

Our finite, minds which have sinned since the age of accountability, cannot comprehend the beauty of the human bodies Adam and Eve had before they sinned. Their fellowship with God was perfect. HE created them; HE gave them the beautiful Garden of Eden as their home; and HE talked with them person-to-person. Satan knew all this before he approached them. Much has been written about how beautiful Satan was in the Garden of Eden. He knew how to disguise himself as a creature of real outer beauty and he did. He has not changed - he still disguises himself as something beautiful today; thus he is not so easily recognized as Satan, the arch enemy of Christians.

When We Pray

In American culture today, most people have heard about prayer to God, even if they are not Christians. Most Americans do not object to going to a nice restaurant and sit quietly as the people sitting at a table nearby bow their heads as someone offer a short prayer of thanks for their food. This is one of the blessings of being an American.

In other situations it is not so easy to pray. As children grow from elementary school to middle school and beyond, praying in every circumstance is not easy. Our seventh and eighth-graders get interested in sports. They rush home from school or a parent picks them up at school and takes them immediately on to sports practice. Baseball, basketball, swimming and other sports take up their after-school time.

When the family does get home everyone is exhausted. A family dinner must be prepared. Mothers, who are usually conscientious about their child's nutrition, get frantic about what she can quickly put together to serve the family for dinner. The budget is already strained because of the frequent eat-outs of 'away from home' ball games, and/or visits of out-of-town relatives, who come to see their grandchildren, nieces or nephews etc. compete in school sports. Frozen pizza is a family favorite, but it is neither healthy nor nutritious to eat pizza seven days a week.

The strain is lessened if the mother remembers a hungry family is not as persnickety as a family that has been at home relaxing all day. A wise mother will choose a "quick to fix" meal, buy what is needed for two or three of them and keep at least one on the pantry shelf at all times. If the food budget will cover it, a 'Ready To Eat Frozen Dinner' for every member of the family is an easy solution.

Adults remember many things about their childhood, but the most significant memory is family prayer before eating. They vividly remember the first time that Mother or Father said, "Would you please pray and thank God for our food?" As adults, we know that prayer is talking with God, and we are keenly aware our children will probably never forget the first time they were asked to say a prayer before eating a meal, or saying a prayer with the family before bedtime.

How We Pray

"Lord, teach us to pray (Luke 11:1)." Had they been with Jesus all this time and never heard Him pray? Why not? It is truly believed that Jesus prayed often and really in a mind-set of prayer all the time He was with His disciples. The inference is He prayed silently, not audibly until this request.

Length of a prayer is not important to God, but it seems to be important to most adults who lead public prayers. We seem to forget that Jesus' prayer, *"Father forgive them for they know not what they do, (Luke 23:34)"* is not a lengthy prayer", but it is vital to know this about our Savior. He is a Savior who forgives the greatest of sins when forgiveness is asked or begged for according to God's instruction.

Because of this some people think Jesus taught that lengthy prayers are not acceptable to God. This is not the context; the context is 'a sinful desire to be known for our long, beautifully worded prayers.' When I was in labor with my first baby, my husband sat by my bedside for the fifteen or so hours and prayed and cried through every long, hard pain. Out of concern for him I tried not to 'let on' but the last three hours before our daughter was born were spent with him crying and praying for me and me screaming, moaning and me begging God for relief (loud praying).

When one meditates about Jesus' foreknowledge of His death on the cross, we begin to get a more appreciative knowledge of not only His love for all mankind, but the heinousness of sin before God; and the emotional cost of forgiveness for God to give His Son as our ransom for our sins.

Jesus is the Son of God: He knew the future; He knew how excruciating His death on the cross was going to be before He came to earth; He knew His sinless life was the only payment pure enough to cover all our sins.

Our task, while living here on earth, is to learn about our God, His Son Jesus, and let the Holy Spirit comfort us through life's trials and hardships. Keep our confidence in them, and they will not fail us.

Chapter 2

Homework Assignment

Write a short prayer suitable for you to give a new Christian woman that will help her learn to pray. Stress daily prayer will help her to grow in the Lord.

Example:

Dear Father in heaven. I come to you knowing that I have sinned and am confident the blood of your Son, Jesus, has cleansed me from my sin. Please help me to:

1. Always keep in mind that I became a Christian
2. Read the Bible every day when possible.
3. Learn to pray asking forgiveness for my sins before YOU - being confident that YOU will forgive.
4. Keep in mind if YOU, God have forgiven me, I must learn not to let the memory of these forgiven sins constantly weigh me down.
5. Pray - "YOU, God have forgiven my sins, please help me to remember when YOU forgive, YOU forget; therefore when someone sins against me I, too, must forgive and forget."
6. Be kind to the offender until my heart truly has learned to forgive the offense.

Keep in mind constantly that Christianity is a lifetime learning process. No Christian is perfect. Most non-Christians do not realize this and expect sinless perfection from Christians. Remember, the only person who lived a perfect life here on earth was Jesus.

Chapter 3

LIFE'S CHANGES

Spiritual Self-examination

1. How Much Of This Situation Is My Own Fault?

Circle where you are on this scale.

1...2...3...4...5...6...7...8...9...10

Do I need to repent and pray for forgiveness for my own sins
which helped create much of the pain in this situation?

2. "I prayed about this situation and God answered the way He
wanted, but did not answer the way I wanted."

3. What Type Of Prayer Do I Need To Pray?

Check One

Petition for need............{ }

Intercession for others.........{ }

Write your prayer:

Date_____

_____
_____
_____
_____
_____
_____
_____
_____
_____
_____

_____

Your signature

Welcome Changes

Among all of my family, friends and acquaintances, there is only one who won Publisher's Clearinghouse. WOW! How it changed her life! How she welcomed the change! She now had money to travel, money to buy a new car, money to update her wardrobe, money to give gifts to her children, and on and on. No more money problems in her life. Money! Money! Money! Everyone knew that she had money. Money is hard to hide if you win Publisher's Clearinghouse.

The welcome changes most of us experience are not so dramatic. We welcome a new baby; our husbands, sons or we, ourselves get promotions and salary increases. We buy a new home. We trade in the old clunker and get a really shiny new car. Now there is money to treat ourselves by eating out occasionally.

But what happened to the peaceful existence we had before the promotion and raise? We argue over where to go to eat. Someone in the family is angry all through the evening because they did not want to go to that particular restaurant. The children spill their take home plates all over the back seat of the new car. Your husband questions you, "Why did you have to have a new outfit just to go to this restaurant to eat tonight?" Then he turns into the driveway with a flourish so that the neighbors in their yard next door are sure to notice his shiny new car.

***

Unwelcome Changes

Unwelcome changes usually adversely affect our ego. If we are fired from a job we were proud of; had to buy a less expensive home than we really wanted; or our children made lower grades in school or college. Any change that causes us to be embarrassed is an unwelcome change. We begin to blame someone else or make unreasonable excuses for why this change happened. Our humility before God grows a quantum leap if we are able to accept a blow to our ego humbly.

A painful divorce or the death of someone close to us always changes our life forever. Nothing can bring about life as it was before these things happened. The death of a child always brings extremely drastic emotional changes in one's life. Nothing affects a person's outlook on life as much as grief.

No human on earth; whatever their ethnic background or religious faith, is ever free from unwelcome changes. Pitiful indeed are those who must face these unwelcome changes without the avenue of prayer to an all powerful God, who is able and will help them.

***

Something to Do:

Deliberately change something in your usual routine, such as putting off doing the laundry until tomorrow, or instead of serving the usual chicken casserole for dinner tonight, make a pot roast. Not only will your routine be changed, but your family will be so surprised. Take this opportunity to open a discussion about life's changes, and how to adapt without being greatly upset.

***

Something to Think About:

Write about a welcome or unwelcome change in your past life. How you have learned that the change was for your good and it made you a better person.

_____

_____

_____

Prayer Opportunities:

Consider how prayer has affected changes –welcome and unwelcome – which have occurred in your life and the life's of your family and close friends.

_____

_____

_____

***

Notes

Chapter 4

BURNED OUT

Spiritual Self-examination

1. How Much Of This Situation Is My Own Fault?

Circle where you are on this scale.

1...2...3...4...5...6...7...8...9...10

Do I need to repent and pray for forgiveness for my own sins which helped create much of the pain in this situation?

2. Does this apply? Be honest in your answer.

"I prayed about this

and God answered the way He wanted,

but did He not answer the way I wanted."

3. What Type Of Prayer Do I Need To Pray ?

Check One

Petition for need............{ }

Intercession for others..........{ }

Write your prayer:

Date_____

_____

_____

_____

_____

_____

_____

_____

_____

_____

_____

_____

Your signature

What Causes "Burn Out?"

The problems in life are relentless! As soon as one is solved, there looms another even more difficult. If you are a salesperson, the main office will keep raising your sales quota. If you are a teacher, your performance ratings depend on the year end tests of your students. If you are a stay-at-home mom, your house is rarely clean and in order. Your children need to improve their grades, but how to be successful in getting them to do their homework and not become a 'Screaming Mom?' Your husband is tired of your weekly routine of most main dishes made with ground beef. He is as nice about it as can be, but he is burned out eating ground beef!

A young Christian woman, who did not finish high school until she was married and had four children, decided to get an education in order to be a better servant of God. She went to night school to earn a GED high school diploma. Then she enrolled in college, worked constantly to earn a Bachelor's Degree in Biology. When she applied for a teaching position, she was told she would be hired on the condition she begin immediately to work on a master's degree and have it completed in three years. She taught school in the daytime and went to the university at night and on Saturdays. She had heard of the term 'Burned Out,' but by the time she was awarded her Master's Degree, she experienced inside out and sideways the true meaning of 'Burned Out.'

One of the worst by-products of being burned out is to feel this has happened to 'you alone.' No one truly understands how tired you really are. Even if your best friend describes herself as "Burned Out," a person secretly feels and does not say " ...not as tired as I am." Even talking about your feelings makes you feel more burned out.

It has been thought by many women as they sit on the pew in an assembly of the saints, "I do not think any woman here is as tired as I am! ... has as messy a house as I have!...has teenagers that are driving her crazy... or a boss as demanding as mine! I am truly too burned out to function much longer! What can I do to better my situation?"

Help Suggestion Number One: *God understands…*HE made you; others may sympathize, but Your Creator knows that you are not perfect. HE understands and will not judge you harshly.

Help Suggestion Number Two: *Praise God in song*! Singing will release tension. No need to sing to the top of your voice, but sing several worship songs. Praising God in song brings healing to the soul.

Help Suggestion Number Three: *Make your TO DO list shorter*: Do only the truly necessary things. Sometimes this is not possible… children cannot wait. They need a functional Mom. Take drastic action! The 'student wife and mother' talked about earlier cut out watching television in the evenings. As the children and their father watched their favorite shows, she stayed in a bedroom - first doing a daily Bible reading, then studying textbooks.

This change did not totally keep her from feeling 'burned out,' but helped her enormously. She grew closer to God because reading the Bible was done before studying college textbooks. When a person is reading the Bible, he/she has a different mind-set about "I am so-o-o-tired." Almost every great Biblical hero or heroine suffered from being "Burned Out."

When a Bible hero or heroine 'burned out' he/she usually took matters into their own hands and made great problems for their lives, i.e., Adam and Eve, Abraham and Sarah, Jonathan and King Saul. Pray and ask God for wisdom as to how to relieve your situation. Keep on keeping on! Someone has said that the most encouraging words in the Bible are, "And it came to pass."

***

Something to Do:

Think about someone you know who has greater problems than you.
Pray earnestly that God will relieve his/her situation.

***

Something to Think About:

Write a three sentence plan that you can do to relieve
the overwhelming feeling of being burned out.

_____

_____

_____

Notes

Chapter 5
FINANCIAL PROBLEMS

Spiritual Self-examination

1. How Much Of This Situation Is My Own Fault?

Circle where you are on this scale.

1…2…3…4…5…6…7…8…9…10

Do I need to repent and pray for forgiveness for my own sins which helped create much of the difficulty in handling this problem?

2. Does this apply? Be honest in your answer.

"I prayed about this

and God answered the way He wanted,

but did not answer the way I wanted?

What Type Of Prayer Do I Need To Pray?

Check One

Petition for need…………{ }

Intercession for others……….{ }

Write your prayer:

Date_____

_____

_____

_____

_____

_____

_____

_____

_____

_____

_____

_____

Your signature

Financial Problems

Most marriage counselors agree the number one issue that triggers arguments between husbands and wives is finances:

"You paid what for that dress?!"
"What do you mean; you need a bigger allowance for food?!"
"We can drive that perfectly good car for another year!"
"Go to another dentist, braces do not have to be so expensive!"
"Get real; we cannot afford Disneyland this year!"

By the time the couple gets though the 'lean years' of a marriage, their habit of arguing about money is a fixed habit. A habit so ingrained in their relationship it has become normal behavior. Their sons and daughters have listened to 'money fusses' all of their lives. Inadvertently, they model this same behavior when they marry.

Money causes the same attitude in almost every human living - now or has ever lived before. There is never enough! Young married couples want to have more money - ten thousand dollars a year more would be enough. Success in business gives them ten thousand dollars a year more, but then they want more. The world's richest billionaires want another billion.

The first step in living on one's income is to list everything that is spent. Everything means everything; cokes at work, ice cream, treats for the children, and the major items such as house and car payments.

Second step is to go to the library and check out several books about living on one's income. There are so many books written on this subject that one may think there is magic success in merely reading the books. Reading books will not manage your income.

Third step is to choose a plan and then without deviation, *work the plan!* Self-discipline and determination are pushed almost beyond human limits when working the plan. It is extremely difficult to get out of debt when the monthly income cannot make every payment on time every month.

Emergencies will happen sometimes to upset the plan. If your son or daughter has an accident going to or from school, the extra expenses will have to be put into your budget causing an even more Spartan lifestyle for you and your family. Be determined! Adjust your budget even more stringently. An unplanned pregnancy will certainly cause a re-working of the family budget. Even if you have good medical insurance, there will be extra expenses. A small fender-bender with $500.00 deductable insurance will put an additional strain on the family budget.

Stay home more and play family games with the children. Monopoly and card games are lots of fun for your children. When they become adults, they will fondly remember these family play times. Of course, they will remember there was little money, but the real blessing is they remember their parents loved them enough to play with them.

Expect the agony of getting out of bed every morning knowing you will have to do without something you really enjoy in order to get out of debt. No stopping at Starbucks for coffee; a sack lunch instead of going to the local cafeteria for lunch.

An Olympic athlete is tremendously disciplined twenty four-seven striving to win a gold medal. When you get your debts where you can make your monthly payments and have enough money for a movie or splurge to take you family out to dinner occasionally, you will be as happy as any gold medal winner.

Something to Do:

Be faithful about keeping good records of each dollar you spend getting out of debt. Pray daily for strength to stay with this regimen until all debts are under control.

Something to Think About:

Be careful not to talk about your plan as an "expert" who knows how to get things done. You can talk like an expert *after your debts are under control.*

_____
_____
_____

Notes

Chapter 6

MY RESPONSIBILITY TO GOD

Spiritual Self-Examination

1. I need to know exactly what my responsibility
to God is, but I am not sure that I do.

Circle where you are on this scale.

1...2...3...4...5...6...7...8...9...10

Do I need to repent and pray for forgiveness for my own sins which
have blinded me from the clarity of my own responsibility to God?

2. Does this apply? Be honest in your answer.

I prayed about this situation and God answered the way

He wanted, but did He not answer the way I wanted.

3. What Type Of Prayer Do I Need To Pray ?

Check one.

Petition for need............{ }

Intercession for others.........{ }

Write your prayer:

Date_____

_____

_____

_____

_____

_____

_____

_____

_____

_____

_____

_____

Your signature

Talents I Use Now

Ability to talk

Every person who knows about the great God of the universe wonders from time to time what is his/her responsibility to HIM?

Also, almost everyone has had an experience in his/her life when almost subconsciously he/she has breathed desperately "Oh God, please help me!" These experiences do not make a person different from anyone else. These experiences show each and every one of us believes in God, but most of us have never explored exactly what our responsibility is to HIM.

One of the most common expressions in America is, "Oh my God!" When we see:

> Suddenly we have a flat tire.
> We spill a full glass of milk or any other liquid.
> There is a dark spot on our most dressy outfit.
> We forgot to feed the dog before leaving for work.

As Christians we know that God is too sacred for humans to carelessly use this expression. If we are calling on HIM in prayer, this expression is totally appropriate, because HE is our GOD personally. Great care is to be taken in using any expression that becomes a slang expression to be used by everyone, including atheists, as by-words.

God has not left us clueless as to what HE considers our responsibility to HIM.

He has showed you Oh man what is good.
And what does the LORD require of you?
To act justly and to love mercy
and to walk humbly with your God.

Micah 6:8

Developing Unused Talents

Most Christians do not curse or speak off-color words. They keep their language clean. However, sometimes we are not conscious of the fact that 'teasing' using snide remarks hurt people's feelings and harm our relationship to God because we are not thoughtful and kind to others."Susie, I knew you were here today when I saw the pineapple upside cake was just a little too brown on the top. You always make it that way."

Susie did not retort with a loud harsh-word argument, but her spirit was wounded too much to really enjoy the get-together. She could have retorted, "Your bean salad needs better quality beans in it! You used the cheapest on the shelf!" But she did not because Susie, like most Christians, has worked hard on cultivating the talent of being even-tempered.

When one does not develop the talent of empathizing with others and complimenting them on their accomplishments; their speech reveals their thinking. They have become snide and cynical. It takes a strong will and strict self-discipline to develop a talent of being and speaking sympathetic and loving words. One's speech reveals one's heart. Snide sentences come easily, and may sound sophisticated to some, but they destroy the speaker's humility. Those remarks say, "I am selfish and everyone must recognize me as the "BEST!" As Christians, we are commanded to use our talents, but little can really be accomplished until one develops the talent of speaking humbly, mercifully, thus encouraging others with our speaking and being encouraging in our speech.

The Bible commands us to be giving and helpful to the poor, to love our neighbors as ourselves, but this cannot be accomplished until we cultivate the talent of clean speech. When this is learned, thoughtful and loving deeds are much easier to do.

Something to Do:

Make a list of your talents, be honest. You know you have some that you use more than others.

***

Something to Think About:

Most of us associate quietness as humility. Moses was the most humble man on earth (Exodus 12:1), but he never hesitated to speak up when something needed to be said. It is believed because of this quality, God used him to be the leader to guide the Israelites out of Egyptian bondage.

_____

_____

_____

Notes

Chapter 7

OVERCOMING SHYNESS

Spiritual Self-examination

1. How Much Of This Situation Is My Own Fault?

Circle where you are on this scale.

1...2...3...4...5...6...7...8...9...10

Do I need to repent and pray for forgiveness for my own sins which helped create much of the pain in this situation?

2. I prayed about this situation and God answered the way He wanted, but did He not answer the way I wanted.

3. What Type Of Prayer Do I Need To Pray About This Situation?

Check one.

Petition for need............{ }

Intercession for others.........{ }

Write your prayer:

Date_____

_____
_____
_____
_____
_____
_____
_____
_____
_____

_____

Your signature

Shy is defined: Sensitively timid, reserved, and or bashful.

Some women who are shy actually become sick when a situation happens and they need to speak up. If a shy woman is asked to lead a prayer in Ladies' Bible Class, she almost becomes unglued. Her voice shakes as she pleads softly asking for someone else to please pray in her place.

Shyness is not to be confused with submissive. Both are painful. Submissive to one's husband or to the elders is God's command. It takes real desire to please God for a woman to be submissive to her own husband. This is part of the curse for Eve's sin in the Garden of Eden. Both men and women are to be submissive to the elders who rule over in the local congregation.

When visitors attend her congregation for the first time, she is so shy that she cannot walk up to them with a smile on her face and welcome them. She waits until someone who has an out-going personality talks to them to help them feel welcome.

Learning How To Meet and Relate to People

Alone in the privacy of her home she can pretend she is welcoming a visitor and say in a moderately-loud, but pleasant voice, "Hello! We are so happy that you visited with us today. Are you new in the area?" We are a friendly congregation; you will feel right at home with us."

It takes time and will power to learn something new. Remember in school how much time and work it was to memorize an assigned poem when you were a student in school? If you did not spend enough time learning the words, you stammered and did poorly when asked to recite. But if you learned in thoroughly at home, you may have had shaky legs and been greatly relieved when it was over, but you recited it well and received an A or B.

Some of us were born shy and some of us were born to be gregarious. "I was born shy," cannot be a valid excuse for not meeting visitors. God knows your personality. He will reward you for your effort to overcome shyness. We are commanded to be hospitable and to entertain strangers. *Do not forget to entertain strangers, for by so doing some people have entertained angels without knowing it.* (Hebrews *13:2)*

All Christian women have certain behavioral habits they must change to please God. Women who talk too much must work on staying quiet. Believe me this is really difficult! Many times in the car on the way home from worship, the talkative woman beats herself mentally, "Now why did I say that?? I hope that she/he does not take offense. When will I learn to keep my mouth shut when this subject is brought up?" Every Christian woman has to obey God's commands. Welcoming strangers is one of those times when we must speak up.

Your children will be blessed even as they see you working on your shyness problem. If at this point in their lives they have developed a shyness habit, they can learn from you as you struggle to overcome it. When they become adults, they will be better equipped to live in the adult world because they do not struggle with a shyness problem.

Something to Do:

On a sheet of paper write the numbers one to ten. Then think about your own personality. There is a difference between "I just do not like to meet strangers" and being painfully shy. "I just do not like to meet strangers," is number one. Work up to ten. "I literally get sick at my stomach, stutter and almost weep when I must talk with a stranger." Where do you put yourself on this scale? Every woman fits somewhere on it. You do not have to tell anyone about your rating. This can be your secret.

Something to Think About:

If you made a high score on your shyness rating, do not let this become a sin because you boast about your rating. Christian women must be humble. However, if you had a low score of four or under, get some help with your problem. There is help out there. Local colleges have speech classes; take a course in Public Speaking. Join a women's club and meet strangers who are not in your circle of acquaintances. God will bless you for your efforts. You can overcome shyness!

_____

_____

_____

Notes

Chapter 8

ANXIETY IN THE WORKPLACE

Spiritual Self-examination

1. How Much Of This Situation Is My Own Fault?

Circle where you are on this scale.

1...2...3...4...5...6...7...8...9...10

Do I need to repent and pray for forgiveness for my own sins which helped create much of the pain in this situation?

2. Does this apply.? _____(answer yes or no)

I prayed about this situation and God answered the way He wanted to, but did He not answer the way I wanted.

3. What Type Of Prayer Do I Need To Pray About This Situation?

Check One

Petition for need............{ }

Intercession for others..........{ }

Write your prayer:

Date_____

_____

_____

_____

_____

_____

_____

_____

_____

_____

_____

Your signature

The Boss is Too Demanding

There are some work situations that are miserable. Many Christian women are trapped in such work-places because their families truly need the additional income. If your boss is too demanding, many times there is not much you can do about it. Your problems are complicated because co-workers do not like you and are always running to the boss and telling something on you whether true or false. Always keep this in mind… "The boss has not fired me, I must be doing something right!"

One solution is to look for another job. This is not as easy as it sounds. When interviewed for another job, the person or company who interviews you will check your work record and possibly talk with your boss. If the boss does not like you, he/she will not recommend you. Then you are stuck and your boss-employee relationship will be even more strained.

This is a problem where only God can do something to relieve your situation. Trust Him, He will do something if you pray fervently, and in your heart forgive the boss and co-workers for offenses done to you. Treat the boss with Christian courtesy and work as diligently on the job as you would if the boss really was your good friend.

Most of us are short on patience, but God has used trials such as these to teach His people to wait on Him. God may not reveal His purpose for allowing you to be in such an unpleasant situation, but as you know from your Bible studies, He uses situations such as this as tests of our spirituality. If your co-workers do not like you because the boss does not like you, nothing but a humble Christian example will win them over.

Five principles to remember:

1. *Never complain to any co-worker about your work situation.*
2. *If you learn that something they are saying is true, do your best to correct it in a friendly humble manner.*
3. *Arrive a bit early for work and be among the last to leave. This will cut down on the time employees have to get together and talk*

badly about you. They will not say as many bad things about you because of your presence.

4. *When and if the boss calls you in to tell you what you are doing wrong, politely accept the criticism and silently pray for the ability to keep your mouth shut. He is the boss and loudly defending yourself will only add fuel to the fire. Remember to give someone 'a piece of my mind' reduces your mental capacity in their eyes and hurts you more than the ones to whom you are speaking.*

5. *If you do find employment somewhere else, do not 'burn your bridges behind you.' Your main goal is to live a Christian life and Christians do not sever relationships to gratify the desire to get even. Leave graciously and do not talk about your bad situation in your new place of employment.*

Something to Do:

Bake a batch of cookies or cupcakes. After they cool, put them on a stiff paper plate and cover with clear plastic wrap. Take them to the nearest fire station or police station from your home. Tell the personnel there how much you appreciate how they make your community a safer and better place to live. The boss may not like you, but these city employees will be all smiles and your morale will get a big boost.

Something to Think About:

Those who work in nursing homes caring for the elderly have said to me privately, "The patients who get the most visitors are the patients who get the most attention from the ones who work there." Visit the local nursing home and inquire what you can do to make their lives better. On the third or fourth regular visit, you will find that in this place you are really appreciated. Do not do this for show, and keep in mind the patients' welfare. I repeat: The boss may not like you, but when you are in that nursing home, you will be loved and appreciated.

_____

_____

_____

Notes

Chapter 9
HELP ME BE A SOUL-WINNER

Spiritual Self-examination

1. How Much Of This Situation Is My Own Fault?

Circle where you are on this scale.

1...2...3...4...5...6...7...8...9...10

Do I need to repent and pray for forgiveness for my own sins which helped create much of the pain in this situation?

2. Does this apply? Be honest in your answer.

I prayed about this situation and God answered the way

He wanted to, but did He not answer the way I wanted.

3. What Type Of Prayer Do I Need To Pray About This Situation?

Check One or two or both

Petition for need...........{ }

Intercession for others.........{ }

Write your prayer:

Date_____

_____

_____

_____

_____

_____

_____

_____

_____

_____

_____

_____

Your signature

Soul-Winning At Home

Examine your normal routine. Find a time - about thirty minutes; steadfastly make this as your soul-winning time. Call a non-Christian and start a conversation about eternal things. Take a non-Christian neighbor a plate of cookies with a tract that tells "How to Become A Christian." If she asks you to come in and stay a while, decline her invitation and go home. This will keep you on track for your reason for the visit. Make another call the next week and ask her about her church home. Do not stay a long time, make your visit short.

If you are a "stay-at-home Mom," telephone her and ask her to come to your house for mid-morning coffee. Find interests that you two have in common. This may be a little difficult if she frequents bars and has only non-Christian friends.

Is there a neighborhood park near you? A short time later in your friendship, you can take the children to the park to play while you two discuss Bible verses. Do not be too pushy, but do not be such a coward that she does not know why you are a Christian or why she needs to be a Christian.

In the meantime, you probably will have unmade beds and laundry that piles up. God will provide a time for you to catch up. However, on Judgment Day Jesus will not talk about your unmade beds and dirty dishes. He will ask, "Did you *'Go into all the world and teach the Gospel to every creature?'* " (*Mark 16:15*)

If you are a dedicated Soul-Winner, your children will reap great benefits because of your example. Jesus will become more real to them in their lives.

Soul Winning Abroad

Teaching the Bible by correspondence course can be done by any woman who can read. World Bible School provides names and the lessons are not very expensive. The real expense is in the postage to mail something overseas. Start small with a few students. When and if you get too many asking you for Bible lessons, ask your sisters in Christ to help you. There really is only one thing to can get you in a mess – is sending American money to foreign people. Then you get requests for money and not for the Word of God.

If you can schedule three or four weeks off to go on a mission trip with a missionary, do so. If you do not have enough money to go, your home congregation will help you from the church treasury. These trips change lives for eternity. Some of the ones you teach will become Christians and teach others about Jesus.

You will never be the same after going on a mission trip. Your perspective on material things will be changed. If it is not possible for you to go, help your teen aged children to go. They will bless you for the rest of their lives for the opportunity.

If you or none in your family are able to go, reduce the entertainment allotment in your budget and give a few dollars to help someone else go. When they return and give their reports to the congregation, your soul will be thrilled and it will say to you, "…And I helped!!!"

Something to Do:

Get a foreign-Exchange student in your home for six months to a year. He/she will attend worship services with you and become acquainted with the others in church. In time they will learn the Gospel and how Christians live in their homes. You do not need to be young to have children in your home. Some agencies let grandparents take these students into their homes.

Something to Think About:

Take time from your busy schedule and think about your life if you had never heard the Gospel and how to be saved. Large popula- tions of real people today truly have never heard the Gospel.

Write your thoughts.

_____

_____

_____

Notes

Chapter 10

PARENTING ISSUES

Spiritual Self-examination

1. How Much Of This Situation Is My Own Fault?

Circle where you are on this scale.

1...2...3...4...5...6...7...8...9...10

Do I need to repent and pray for forgiveness for my own sins which helped create much of the difficulty in handling this problem?

2. Does this apply? Be honest in your answer.

"I prayed about this

and God answered the way He wanted to,

but did He not answer the way I wanted.

3. What Type Of Prayer Do I Need To Pray?

Check One

Petition for need............{ }

Intercession for others.........{ }

Write your prayer:

Date_____

_____
_____
_____
_____
_____
_____
_____
_____
_____
_____

_____

Your signature

Newborn Baby

The doorbell rang and the weary, sleep-deprived mother of a three week old baby carried her infant in her arms as she went to open the front door. She was expecting her mother to come to see her new grandbaby, but she never dreamed her mother would react to her daughter's appearance as she did.

Her mother took the baby in her arms, kissed it and said sternly to her daughter. "Go to bed! Get some sleep! I will take care of this baby for a while. I mean it, go to bed!" Then the daughter realized how pitiful she really looked with her eyes bloodshot, needing a shower because she had not had one for two days, and how much her mother understood her desperate need for sleep; and how deeply her mother loved her. She gave the baby to its grandmother and went to bed and slept for fourteen wonderful hours with no interruptions.

When she woke up the next morning, mother had made breakfast and the baby was wide awake in good humor in her bassinet. As she sipped her coffee, she told her mother how she had said to her husband only three days ago, "I know that we have no money to get someone to help me with this colicky newborn baby, but if we could afford it, I would pay a reliable person $500.00 to watch this baby for one night so I could get a good night's sleep.

Adolescent

It has been noted that the reason our children have such a difficult time in their adolescence is because their parents were their idea of 'perfection' when they were infants, toddlers, and in grade school. During the onset of adolescence, they begin to see that their parents have real character flaws. "Nobody is perfect" is easy for them to accept about their parents later in life; but when 'Parental Perfection' loses its halo, adolescents consider this to be an open door for them to do as they please, and 'Imperfect Parents' do not have the right to be their bosses anymore.

They do not realize that parents worry more, cry more, pray more, and sometimes get to the place where they want to give up and let the adolescent do their thing and suffer the consequences. The best thing for parents to do is remember the words of Winston Churchill and never give up. Their well-trained child will get through this phase of life and become a wonderful adult.

Experienced police officers who write speeding citations expect the guilty speeder to lie to his/her parents and claim the officer was 'out to get them' because he/she knew they had authority. There may be a few renegade policepersons who are this way, but they are a tiny minority in police work. Because the parents want to believe their child, many fall into this adolescent.

The Strong-Willed Child

Parents who have a strong-willed child are advised to seek professional help. There are many counselors to whom they can go for advice. It is a treacherous and slippery slope to 'go it on your own' with a strong willed child.

Seek the counsel of the elders in your congregation first. They may be able to counsel with your child and that will be the end of it. If there is a truly serious behavioral problem, they will be able to refer you to reliable professional help. You are not alone. Reliable help is available. After your child reaches adulthood, he/she will thank you for getting help.

Something to Do:

Start today to train yourself not to see or take note of anyone's messy house. There is an art to this, because women who are messy housekeepers tune in immediately that a visitor sees everything is out of place. Your visit can and will be ruined by roving 'Inspector Eyes.'

Something to Think About:

Take a look at the time before calling mothers of young children; because phone calls during nap times are sometimes so disruptive of the napping children the true concern which inspired the phone call is lost. Children who did not get a full-time nap are fussy for the rest of the day.

Notes

Chapter 11

How To Be A Better Bible Student

Spiritual Self-examination

1. How Much Of This Situation Is My Own Fault?

Circle where you are on this scale.

1...2...3...4...5...6...7...8...9...10

Do I need to repent and pray for forgiveness for my own
sins of omission which helped create this situation?

2. Does this apply? Be honest in your answer.

How many times have I asked

God in prayer to help me be a better Bible student?

3. What Type Of Prayer Do I Need To Pray About This Situation?

Does this apply, petition for more time in my
schedule for prayer and Bible study?

Write your prayer:

Write your prayer:

Date_____

_____
_____
_____
_____
_____
_____
_____
_____
_____
_____

_____

Your signature

Make a Regular Reading Time Every Day

Making a regular time every day to is the most difficult part of accomplishing this goal. Satan will use every disruption in his catalogue to cause this to not get done. The Bible says: *"Do your best to present yourself to God as one approved a workman who does not need to be ashamed and one who correctly handles the word of truth"*

(II Timothy 2:15).

It is impossible for a person who does not know the alphabet to read a book. Learning the alphabet is essential to learning to read. In the same manner, it is impossible for a person to learn very much about the Bible until they learn about the difference between the Old Testament and the New Testament.

The beginning Bible scholar must learn that the first four books of the New Testament are Matthew, Mark, Luke, and John and they are the books that tell about Jesus' life when HE came to earth. Reading these carefully and prayerfully is the starting point toward good scholarship in the Bible.

Do not give up! Do not quit because something happened in your life that caused you to miss reading the Bible for a time. If you have a severe illness or surgery, which hinders you from reading the Bible every day, do not become discouraged and say, "Oh well!, God knows I tried, but it did not work out." Expect some hindrances, but make sure in your own mind that you are going to keep on keeping on reading the Bible every day if at all possible. Weak excuses make the 'workman ashamed' before God. Always be aware that God is all knowing, HE knows if your reason is valid or a weak excuse.

There are many words in the Bible that are difficult to pronounce. Your reading will be so much easier if you get a recording of someone reading the Bible and listen to it as you read silently. Continue to read silently with the recording until you learn the message of the passage and can pronounce the words correctly.

Attend a Bible study class regularly. Listen to their reading aloud and their discussions. Always keep foremost in your mind that the Bible is God's inspired word. God has commanded that people study it in order to learn how to be and to stay in covenant relationship with HIM.

You will be pleasantly surprised to see, after a short period of time reading the Bible every day, you will have learned enough about certain passages you can join in class discussions with a good amount of knowledge. After a few classes you will look forward to being with others who are also eager to read the Bible. God will bless you and you will become aware HE is blessing you. There is no greater happiness on earth than being secure in the knowledge that God is blessing you because you study HIS word diligently and have a sustained relationship with HIM.

Reading the Bible every day will change your life. You will learn how to pray, how not to gossip, to give to the poor, and how to love the unlovable and to attend worship services regularly. Your friends will see these changes in you. Some of them will not be as fond of you as they once were because your speech and lifestyle have changed from godless ways to God's holy ways. You will make new friends who are also reading the Bible every day. A richness of your inner spirit, money cannot buy, will bless you constantly.

Choosing Good Non-Biblical Reading Materials

To help strengthen your reading ability, as well as your spirituality, choosing good non-biblical reading material will reinforce your cognitive development. There are many well-known authors who have penned wonderful non-biblical books which focus on wholesome subjects. Reading these type books will help you keep your mind on positive things, i.e., self-improvement, scrapbooking, photography.

However, there are many non-Biblical books written to give the spiritual person needed support with understanding various aspects of God's Word. Look for books written by Christian authors regarding characteristics relative to salvation and Christian living. Look for books to explore such subjects as: Angels, Blessings, Faith, Grace, Holiness, Love, Mercy, Prayer, Righteousness, Salvation, Trust, and Worship.

As the Apostle Paul wrote in his letter to the Philippians: *"Finally brothers, whatever is true, whatever is noble, whatever is right, whatever is admirable – if anything is excellent or praiseworthy – think about such things."* (*Philippians 4: 8*)

Something to Do:

Go to a bookstore and buy an inexpensive, paper-back copy of a Bible designed to be read through in one year. No matter how tired and sleepy you are by bedtime, ***Do Not Go To Sleep Until You Have Read at least One-Half of the Daily Assignment!*** *Remember Satan hates you and God and he will do all he can to keep you from reading the Bible and learning God's will for your life.*

Something to Think About:

Think about Moses taking a pen and parchment, sitting down at some quiet place and writing, "In the beginning God,............" He was following God's dictation. He probably did not know the precious book he began writing that day would be in heaven through- out all eternity. Write a sentence telling what the Bible means to you.

_____

_____

_____

***

Notes

Chapter 12
RESTORING LOVE IN MY MARRIAGE

Spiritual Self-examination

1. How Much Of This Situation Is My Own Fault?

    Circle where you are on this scale.

    1...2...3...4...5...6...7...8...9...10

Do I need to repent and pray for forgiveness for my own sins which helped create much of the pain in this situation?

2. I prayed about this situation and God answered the way He wanted, but did He not answer the way I wanted.

3. What Type Of Prayer Do I Need To Pray?

    Check One

    Petition for need............{ }

    Intercession for others.........{ }

Write your prayer:

Date_____

_____

_____

_____

_____

_____

_____

_____

_____

_____

_____

Your signature

The Difference Between Hollywood Love and True Love

Shortly before one young bride's wedding, her mother sat her down for a heart-to-heart talk. "I know you love him greatly now, but there will be times in your married life you will look at him and say in your heart, "What did I ever see in him? Why did I marry him?" Every woman who has been married for several years knows the young bride's mother was right.

The word *"Always"* seems to be the culprit, which troubles most marriages. If the song, *Always* is sung at the wedding, it brings tears of joy to the eyes of the bride and groom. The word _always_ is beautiful in a song, but a destroyer of good relationships when said to a spouse in anger. She says, "You _always_ wait until the garbage is running over before you take it out!" Or he says, "I _always_ have to wait so long for you to put on your make up and do your hair!"

Both of these complaints may be truly valid, but the poisonous sting is not as deadly when the word _always_ is left out of the sentence. Your true feelings can be spoken and the complaint is validated by a peaceful discussion using reason. "Please do not wait until the garbage is running over before you empty it, sometimes it stains the kitchen floor." or "Will you try to get your make-up and hair done so we can leave early enough to miss the five o'clock traffic?" The Hollywood love story does not have garbage to be taken out or 'bad hair days' when it is impossible to get it to look good, but these things happen in real life.

It seems that perfectionists usually marry 'messy' spouses. 'Early-to-bed' persons marry "stay up late' people; 'meat and potatoes' people marry 'vegetarians.' A successful marriage does not demand that 'stay up late' people must get up early, or vegetarians must eat meat. Lasting marriages result when both parties cultivate tolerance and forbearance and continue to respect their spouses' high quality characteristics.

When a Hollywood actor gets ready to play a difficult part, he/she develops the character of the role 'face first.' If the role is one of a grouch, he/she makes his/her face have a grouchy look. They know the grouchy face will cause the entire body to quickly tense up, and the voice will sound gruff when the lines are read. If the role is one of a sweet 'everybody's best friend' role, the actor puts an 'I love everybody' relaxed smile on his face and reads the lines. The voice will follow the look on the face and 'best friend' wins the affection of the viewing audience.

To have a successful marriage one does not have to become an actor twenty-four-seven, but to keep the conversation on a level where differences can be resolved in a reasonable manner, it helps to force a smile on the face; then begin the conversation as an actor if necessary. A pleasant voice and friendly body language will help get the problem out in the open and find ways to resolve it. *"In your anger do not sin."* (*Ephesians 4:26 NIV*).

Get advice from an older woman who is trustworthy about marital problems. Older women are commanded to teach the younger women to love their husbands and children. They are God's designated persons who are to help the younger women. If you ask an older woman for advice and/or help, she must not gossip to anyone about the problems she is helping a younger woman or many younger women solve.

Married life is not a Hollywood movie. However, there is value in learning how to smile, and speaking in a controlled normal voice. Putting a smile on our faces when we feel like having a temper tantrum toward our spouse to let him know how much we detest certain behaviors never solves any problem. Ugly frowns and high pitched shouting exacerbate problems and make them more difficult and sometimes impossible to solve.

Something to Do:

Sit down with your husband and have a heart-to-heart talk telling him your intentions to do everything in your power to help your relationship to be God-Directed. Do not blame him for anything and do not raise your voice in anger.

***

Something to Think About:

"The older people become the more they get set in their ways and cannot change" is an old saying completely different from what the Bible teaches. The Bible commands Christians to constantly strive to become like Christ.

Write a behavior you are going to change to improve your marriage relationship.

_____

_____

_____

Notes

Chapter 13

A Single Woman In a Couples World

Spiritual Self-examination

1. How Much Of This Situation Is My Own Fault?

Circle where you are on this scale.

1...2...3...4...5...6...7...8...9...10

Do I need to repent and pray for forgiveness for my own sins which helped create much of the pain in this situation?

2. "I prayed about this situation and God answered the way He wanted to, but did He not answer the way I wanted."

3. What Type Of Prayer Do I Need To Pray ?

Check One

Petition for need...........{ }

Intercession for others.........{ }

Write your prayer:

Date_____

_____

_____

_____

_____

_____

_____

_____

_____

_____

_____

Your signature

The Unmarried Woman

After a single female graduates from high school, she is considered an unmarried woman. If she goes to college, she is expected to find a mate during her college years. If she does not attend a college, but goes immediately to work, i.e. as a waitress, or in a factory, she is considered an unmarried woman. Society demands she either marry or give an absolutely valid reason why she does not marry. If she remains unmarried by her thirtieth birthday, she is considered an 'old maid.' She may call herself a 'career girl,' but most people will continue to think about her as an old maid. After she becomes forty and is eminently successful, there are fewer comments about her getting married.

There is no Biblical record that Phoebe was married. Her name was mentioned in the Bible only one time. *"I commend to you our dear sister Phoebe, a deaconess in the church at Cenchreae, that you may receive her in the Lord as befits the saints, for she has been a helper of many and of myself as well." (Romans 16:1-2)*

Paul used Phoebe to take the letter he wrote to the Christians at Rome. How many millions have been blessed by reading and studying Paul's letter to the Romans?! Phoebe may not have ever been married or she may have been widowed, the Bible does not tell us. It simply states that she was a helper of many. She was such a helper that Paul encouraged the Christians at Rome to help Phoebe in any work with which she needed help.

This is still true in the Church today. Christian women of all ages are helping people who need help. Most women in the church today are career women. They are not able to do much baking cookies in their own kitchens to help VBS, but they certainly know how to drive their own car to the local bakery and buy dozens of delicious cookies. The job gets done.

They get the job done that needs to be done, without much talk about it. If there is a death, she orders flowers, takes food, gives money to those who need it to get to the funeral. Unmarried Christian women of any age or skin color are the greatest helpers in any time of any kind of need whether great or small.

Widows

There is nothing more heart-rending than a newly widowed woman going to worship on Sunday after burying her loving husband that week. Of course, some in her family will be with her, but her loss is so enormous words are inadequate to describe it. She still loves her children and grand-children dearly, but her heart is so lonely, it is almost unbearable the first Sunday.

There are really no words that will bring solace to her aching heart, but speak them to her anyway. As time goes by the loss will ease, and she will remember the wonderful kind words and deeds done for her when her husband died. As soon as possible she needs to help someone herself. Helping someone is the greatest medicine to ease sorrow.

Something to Do:

The nearest of kin to you will want to accompany you to worship on the first Sunday after your husband's funeral. This custom has become a tradition. After you arrive at the church building:

* Sit in your usual seat.
* Weep as quietly as you can, but do not try to keep from crying.
* Accept hugs from your friends who are mourning with you.
* Let God's love comfort you. God's care and comfort of widows is one of the most prominent threads in the entire Bible. God will not fail you!

Something to Think About:

Think about the desolation that a woman feels when she goes to worship the first Sunday after she knows that her status will be 'Divorcee.' She may sit quietly, but the pain in her heart is inconsolable. Words will not help her as much as you just quietly being there for her. Sit by her quietly, after service if possible, and then perhaps take her and the children (if she has children) to a nice Sunday brunch.

Notes

Part II

ALPHABET
FOR
A PRAYING
CHRISTIAN WOMAN

To study prayer effectively, one must know:

5. Who prayed?
6. What was the purpose of the prayer?
7. How did God answer it?
8. How did it change their life?

**God has not changed;
He will do the same for us today!**

How Can Women Pray and Be Sure God Will Answer?

Guest Writer: Margy (Seay) Murray

Margy (Seay) Murray retired from pecuniary employment in 2007, just before moving to Heber Springs, Arkansas, with her husband, Howard, who is a semi-retired minister and funeral director.

Mrs. Murray is from a family of 14 siblings whose parents were Willie and Thelma (Norman) Seay. After graduating high school (1957), at Lake City, Arkansas, Mrs. Murray attended and graduated from Ouachita Baptist University (1961), Arkadelphia, Arkansas, where she received a Bachelor of Arts degree in Secretarial Science. She taught business subjects for three years in St. Charles and Des Arc, Arkansas. Mrs. Murray then attended one year at Southwestern Baptist Theological Seminary in 1964, where she met her future husband, Howard. They married on May 22, 1965.

Mrs. Murray worked as a secretary while her husband finished his seminary training. The couple then moved to her husband's first pastorate in Bethlehem, Pennsylvania in 1967. During her years as a minister's wife, Mrs. Murray taught Bible lessons for all ages in the several church congregations her husband was employed. She taught Bible classes for children through adults.

Mr. and Mrs. Murray have two children; a daughter, Audra and a son, Nathan, who were born in Bethlehem, Pennsylvania in 1967 and 1970, respectively.

Editor's Note: Due to her background, education, and experience as the wife of a minister and her knowledge as a Bible class teacher, Mrs. Murray was asked to provide a woman's insight regarding the effectiveness of prayers offered to God by a woman. Using examples from her life experiences, Mrs. Murray offers her perception and practice of prayer with ***How Prayer is an Active Part in My Life for the Lord***, as basis for her faith in prayer and God's grace toward those who call upon His name.

How Prayer is an Active Part in My Life for the LORD

By: Marge (Seay) Murray

All through my years as a Christian - starting at nearly age 15 - I have learned how praying about all things has developed my courage and strength to face each day by taking hold of God's willingness of *"not our will but Thy will be done."* It is not, as I hear so many Christians say, "Prayer works," but rather God works *when* we pray. Our main work is to pray. He takes the energy of our prayers to Him and uses that energy to do His work. I've learned prayer is not to be a monologue, but a dialogue (fellowship) with our Lord; prayer is not a ritual to observe in certain circumstances or to be used as a magic lamp to rub to have a desire or need met. It is not to be used as a way of trying to persuade God to get our way. It is not to be used as a labor saving device. As the expression goes, "put feet to our prayers" and do our part to see our prayers answered.

Therefore, we need to always be in an attitude of prayer with our will bent upward to ask that His will be done. As God's children, we should seek His fellowship through prayer beginning with praise to Him and thanksgiving and confession - confession of our wrong doing so, as an example we can pray, "If you find favor with me, Lord, grant that my sister be made well."

In troublesome times, we find ourselves only able to give sighs and groans directed toward God; and the Holy Spirit, in turn, takes our inadequate words to the Lord for us, because Jesus is there at the Father's right hand making intercession for His children.

An example of having to trust the Lord: When I was finishing my last year of college toward graduation, I had to have all my tuition fees paid up. There was a banker friend from back home who had made the commitment to pay my tuition throughout college. It was getting to be the last week and I was to take finals. I became anxious about not having the check there to take care of things. A day or so later, the Budget Director came to let me know they had received the final check. I had been praying for that to happen. Even though, I felt it would come in time, I still had anxiety but just had to trust it to the Lord.

Other experiences with knowing that my prayers were and are answered have been to ask the Lord to show me things. For example, during my first year of teaching school I wasn't able to go check on my Mom when she became ill. Dad was one to never encourage her to go to the doctor but suffer through it. So, knowing that, I would pray, asking the Lord to show me she would be okay. It being a cloudy morning that day while I was getting ready to go teach school, I asked Him to show me the sunshine for awhile and I would know she would be okay. Before leaving the house, I happen to look out the window and saw a bit of sunshine peeking through the clouds. This gave me joy and peace in knowing that He loved me enough to hear and answer my prayer.

Another example was when we decided to move back to Arkansas from Illinois. We found a church to attend and I was asked to teach an adult women's class. I had been going through some depression and adjustments of having to make new friends and really didn't seem to have the heart to put time and energy into preparing to teach. However, I made the commitment and each Sunday I would make myself study and prepare for the class. I would teach the lesson using the Lord's strength. I would use some of my life experiences to illustrate some points. As a few Sundays went on, I would hear some of the ladies say to one another they hated to miss a Sunday because they wanted to be there for my lesson. That was a humbling experience and I knew then it was the Lord teaching through me.

One of the illustrations in my Sunday School class was to tell about us using a U-Haul truck while moving back to Arkansas. I had to drive our car, with Audra driving her own car and Howard driving the truck. We stayed up with each other pretty well until it became dusky dark. Then when it began to get darker, we stopped to eat and then had to get back onto the freeway to head on our way. (Now you will have to use your imagination to visualize this to get the full impact.) I was behind the two of them and because it was dark, the lights on the truck were all I had to watch in order to know I was still near them. Because I could not tell which truck was Howard's by that time, I was just hoping and praying the truck I was trying to keep pace with was his. We were still going through the town and the traffic lights before we came to the exit for the entrance ramp to the freeway. I was caught at a red light, but they had to move on. They both had gotten to the exit/entrance ramp to head back onto the freeway. I was just beside myself trying to make sure I was on the right entrance ramp to get back with them. I still could not be sure that the lights on a truck ahead were Howard's. They finally realized they needed to ensure I was behind them and pulled off on the side of the ramp. When I caught up to them, I saw they had waited for me. I fussed at them for not making sure I was behind them, but at the same time I was so elated I did make the right entrance ramp. Then I realized the Lord had been with me all the time and kept me on the right path. I will never forget this experience. That is why I wanted to relate it to the ladies as encouragement for them the Lord will always be with you to protect and guide your steps.

One last - and not least - especially important answered prayer was the time after our Dad had died. I would go to work and on some days while coming home, I would be in a sad mood and still grieving and missing him. I began to cry one afternoon when arriving home. I asked the Lord to let me dream about my Dad in order to give me His assurance that Dad was, indeed, in Heaven with Him. That very night, I dreamed about Dad being at a place where a group of them were able to go into a pool to swim.

I asked Dad, "Are you going to take a swim?"

"It's too cold." Was Dad's reply.

I said, "They're heating it up and you'll be able to get in soon."

He decided to swim and undressed down to his underwear top and shorts.

The next scene seemed to be Dad back at the table with some of the others. I asked if he enjoyed the swim.

"It was okay, but this guy next to me here took my money while I was gone." Dad exclaimed.

However, Dad was not showing anger nor was the guy showing any guilt like he should have.

I woke up then, thinking about the dream being so strange and wondered what it all meant. I finally concluded that because Dad was not angry – he was known to be quite conservative with his money – and the other man did not show guilt, I thought they must have been in heaven where there are no bad things going on. Dad was being forgiving. It was then that I realized that the Lord had sent me my dream as I had asked. The fact that it was the very same night was assurance enough for me the Lord was helping me with my grief because He knows how we feel since He had to go through all things we ever will. Then I just had to email and write my siblings my dream in order to give them assurance, in case they had any anxiety over where Dad was spending eternity.

To conclude all of this with just one more thing, I always loved singing solos whenever I had the opportunity. I always took the time to plan, practice, and pray for His strength and for God to receive the glory. I would sit in the pew, being anxious to get it over with, and ask for His courage. So, when the time came for me to get up, I would arise and take the first step. I could feel that I was at ease and was able to sing without being shaky, but calm as I sang. I knew the Lord wanted me to sing for Him because of the courage that came over me.

I could add so many things, but this might turn into a book by itself. Let me end with a quote I read somewhere and a scripture:

"We cannot come to really know God if we refuse to learn to pray." *(Author Unknown)*

"How precious, also, are Thy thoughts to me, O GOD! How vast is the sum of them! If I should count them, they would outnumber the sand. When I awake, I am still with Thee." Psalms 139: 17-18, ASV

Alphabet of A Praying Christian Woman

A

Always

*"And surely I am with you **always** to the very end of the age."*

(Matthew 28:20)

When you consider the word "always," as Christ intended while speaking these final words to His disciples, what do you discern from His meaning?

_____

_____

_____

_____

Christ demonstrated His commitment before His birth; during His physical life; through His death; and before He ascended to heaven. What is your opinion of Christ's commitment to you today? How does Christ's commitment affect your purpose in prayer?

_____

_____

_____

_____

Write a sentence about how God _always_ answers prayer, with "Yes," "No," or "Wait a while."

_____

_____

_____

Alphabet of A Praying Christian Woman

B

Blessed

"Blessed is he who comes in the name of the LORD."

(Matthew 21:9)

In what circumstances would a woman prayerfully
present herself as blessed before the Lord?

_____

_____

_____

_____

In your opinion, how can a woman pray and be sure
God is blessed by her prayers and supplications?

_____

_____

_____

_____

Write a sentence about how you and other women
who fervently pray to God have been blessed?

_____

_____

_____

_____

Alphabet of A Praying Christian Woman

C

Comforter

"And I will pray the Father, and he shall give you another
<u>Comforter</u>, that he may abide with you forever;" (John 14: 16)

In your opinion, how is the Comforter (the Holy
Spirit) an essential part of a woman's prayer life?

_____

_____

_____

_____

How is the Comforter a _helper_ in guiding
a woman's thoughts in prayer?

_____

_____

_____

_____

Write a sentence about how the Comforter gives
aid and comfort to the praying woman?

_____

_____

_____

_____

Alphabet of A Praying Christian Woman

D

Dreams

"And he said unto them, Hear, I pray you, this dream
which I have dreamed:" (Genesis 37: 6)

God revealed His will to Joseph through dreams. How does a
faithful prayer life help a woman to find solace in restful dreams?

_____

_____

_____

_____

How often do you dream dreams that coincide with
what you have prayed about? In your opinion, what
did you believe God was revealing to you?

_____

_____

_____

_____

Write a sentence about how your dreamed
dreams may impact your future prayers.

_____

_____

_____

_____

Alphabet of A Praying Christian Woman

E

Earnestly

"For in this we groan *earnestly* desiring to be clothed with our habitation which is from heaven." (2 Corinthians 5: 2)

Describe what is meant by "groan *earnestly*." What is the difference between earnest groaning and insincerely groaning when a Christian prays?

_____

_____

_____

_____

What are the attributes of an *earnest* Christian prayer life?

_____

_____

_____

_____

Write a sentence you consider to show an example
of how a woman can *earnestly* pray to God.

_____

_____

_____

_____

Alphabet of A Praying Christian Woman

F

Faith

"Now *faith* is the substance of things hope for, the evidence of things not seen." (Hebrews 11: 1)

What is the difference between *faith* and hope in the life of a Christian?

_____

_____

_____

_____

What do you consider as evidence of *faith* in
a Christian woman's prayer life?

_____

_____

_____

_____

Write a sentence you consider to be an example of what
faith is and how *faith* can be shown in prayer to God.

_____

_____

_____

_____

Alphabet of A Praying Christian Woman

G

Grace

"My *grace* is sufficient for you, for My strength is made perfect in weakness." (2 Corinthians 12: 9)

Describe what you consider sufficient *grace* and how God applies *grace* toward a Christian.

_____

_____

_____

_____

Explain your understanding of the phrase "My strength is made perfect in weakness" as it applies to the *grace* of God.

_____

_____

_____

_____

Why is *grace* important to a Christian's relationship with Christ?

_____

_____

_____

_____

Alphabet of A Praying Christian Woman

H

Hope

"Now *hope* does not disappoint, because the love of
God has been poured out in our hearts by the Holy
Spirit who was given to us." (Romans 5: 5)

What do you consider the role *hope* has with regard
to faith and grace in the process of salvation?

_____

_____

_____

_____

How does *hope* add strength to a Christian's faith,
prayer life, and their relationship with God.

_____

_____

_____

_____

How is *hope* important to a Christian's daily
interrelationships with others?

_____

_____

_____

_____

Alphabet of A Praying Christian Woman

I

Image

"He is the *image* of the invisible God, the first
born over all creation. *(Colossian*s 1: 15)

Explain what is meant by "the *image* of the invisible *God*."

_____

_____

_____

_____

What are the characteristics of God's *image* as it relates to how man was created in His *image* as referenced in Genesis 1: 26?

_____

_____

_____

_____

How did Christ demonstrate "the *image* of God" through His prayers?

_____

_____

_____

_____

Alphabet of A Praying Christian Woman

J

Joy

"Now may the God of hope fill you with all *joy* and peace in believing, that you may abound in hope by the power of the Holy Spirit." (Romans 15: 13)

What impact does *joy* have upon a Christian's prayer life and relationship with God?

_____

_____

_____

_____

How can you demonstrate *joy* as you pray?

_____

_____

_____

_____

How can a Christian deal with adversity and yet be *joyful* in prayer?

_____

_____

_____

_____

Alphabet of A Praying Christian Woman

K

Knees

"For this reason I bow my *knees* to the Father of
our Lord Jesus Christ." (Ephesians 3: 14)

What is the significance of a Christian bowing
down on their *knees* before God in prayer?

_____

_____

_____

_____

When should a Christian bow on their *knees* before another human?

_____

_____

_____

_____

In your opinion, what does a Christian illustrate in their
attitude when bowing down on their *knees* to pray to
God and when they stand as they pray to God?

_____

_____

_____

_____

Alphabet of A Praying Christian Woman

L

Lamp

"…but the wise took oil in their vessels with
their *lamps."* (Matthew 25: 4)

What do you consider to be a Christian's *lamp*
when approaching God in prayer?

_____

_____

_____

_____

In your opinion, how does a Christian ensure
they have scriptural "oil" in their *lamp*?

_____

_____

_____

_____

Relate an occasion when you felt that your
lamp became low on scriptural "oil."

_____

_____

_____

_____

Alphabet of A Praying Christian Woman

M

Mercy

"Bless be the God and Father of our Lord Jesus Christ,
the Father of *mercies* and God of all comfort."

(2 Corinthians 1: 3)

Without *mercy,* how could a person maintain
a Christian relationship with God?

_____

_____

_____

_____

In your opinion, what role does *mercy* play in the process of salvation?

_____

_____

_____

_____

Write a sentence that describes God's *mercies.*

_____

_____

_____

_____

Alphabet of A Praying Christian Woman

N

Need

"And my God shall supply all my *need* according to His riches in glory forever and ever." (Philippians 4: 19)

According to Paul's letter to the Philippians, when can a Christian expect to have all their *need* supplied?

_____

_____

_____

_____

In your opinion, can a Christian rightfully expect God
to supply a physical *need* as an answer to prayer?

_____

_____

_____

_____

In your opinion, what is the difference
between a *need,* a want, and a desire?

_____

_____

_____

_____

Alphabet of A Praying Christian Woman

O

One

"There is *one* body and *one* Spirit, just as you were called
in *one* hope of your calling." (Ephesians 4: 4)

Explain how a fervent prayer life can increase the
feeling and belief of being as *one* with God?

_____

_____

_____

_____

In your opinion, what is the inclusiveness of the "*one* body and *one* Spirit" in a Christian's prayer life and relationship with God?

_____

_____

_____

_____

In your opinion, why must a Christian maintain
that there is only *one* true God?

_____

_____

_____

_____

Alphabet of A Praying Christian Woman

P

Pray

"Pray without ceasing, in everything give thanks."

(1 Thessalonians 5: 17-18)

Explain how a Christian can be expected to *pray* without ceasing.

_____

_____

_____

_____

In your opinion, how can a Christian always
pray and give thanks in every situation?

_____

_____

_____

_____

Write a sentence explaining how fruitful ceaseless
prayer has improved your relationship with God?

_____

_____

_____

_____

Alphabet of A Praying Christian Woman

Q

Quiet

"Therefore I exhort first of all that supplications, prayers, intercessions, and giving of thanks be made for all men, for kings and all who are in authority, that we may lead a *quiet* and peaceable life in all godliness and reverence."

(1Timothy 2: 1-2)

Explain how the idea of leading a *quiet* and peaceable life aids a Christian to pray without ceasing.

_____

_____

_____

_____

In your opinion, how can a Christian lead "a *quiet* and peaceable life" and still teach the gospel to others?

_____

_____

_____

_____

Write a sentence explaining the importance in developing a Christian spirit by maintaining a *quiet* prayer life?

_____

_____

_____

_____

Alphabet of A Praying Christian Woman

R

Rejoice

"Rejoice in the Lord always. Again I will say *rejoice."* (Philippians 4: 4)

Explain how a Christian can *rejoice* in prayer to God.

_____

_____

_____

_____

In your opinion, how can a Christian lead "a quiet and peaceable life" and "*rejoice* in the Lord always?"

_____

_____

_____

_____

Write a sentence describing an occasion where you *rejoiced* in prayer to God?

_____

_____

_____

_____

Alphabet of A Praying Christian Woman

S

Sanctified

"For both he who *sanctifies* and those who are *sanctified*
are as one, for which reason He is not ashamed
to call them brethren." (Philippians 4: 4)

Explain what is meant by *"sanctified."*

_____

_____

_____

_____

In your opinion, what effect does being sanctified
have upon a Christian relationship with God?

_____

_____

_____

_____

Write a sentence describing how a Christian can be
sanctified and still be involved in an everyday life?

_____

_____

_____

_____

Alphabet of A Praying Christian Woman

T

Thanks

"…giving *thanks* always for things to God the Father in the name of our Lord Jesus Christ," (Ephesians 5: 20)

Why did Paul tell his Ephesians brethren to give *thanks* "in the name of our Lord Jesus Christ?"

_____

_____

_____

_____

In your opinion, what effect does remembering to give *thanks* to the Father have upon a Christian relationship with God?

_____

_____

_____

_____

Write a sentence describing how a Christian can give *thanks* outside of prayer to God.

_____

_____

_____

_____

Alphabet of A Praying Christian Woman

U

Understanding

"I will pray with the spirit and I will also pray with the *understanding*." (1 Corinthians 14: 15)

What are things a Christian woman needs in order to "pray with *understanding?*"

_____

_____

_____

_____

In your opinion, what is your *understanding* of the process of prayer – who and what is involved?

_____

_____

_____

_____

Write a sentence illustrating how a better *understanding* of prayer to God can improve your daily life as a Christian.

_____

_____

_____

_____

Alphabet of A Praying Christian Woman

V

Vigilant

"Continue earnestly in prayer, being *vigilant* in
it with thanksgiving;" (Colossians 4: 2)

In your opinion, what did Paul mean when he wrote to the
Colossian church instructing them to be *vigilant* in pray?"

_____

_____

_____

_____

In your opinion, what is the importance
of having a *vigilant* prayer life?

_____

_____

_____

_____

Considering today's society and the multiplicity of issues
facing women in particular, what are some issues a Christian
woman needs to be *vigilant* about in prayer to God.

_____

_____

_____

_____

Alphabet of A Praying Christian Woman

W

Walk

"As you have therefore received Christ Jesus the
Lord, so *walk* in Him," (Colossians 2: 6)

Express your understanding of the phrase "so *walk* in Him"
relative to the point Paul made in this letter to the Colossians.

_____

_____

_____

_____

How is it possible for a Christian to have a daily *walk* in Christ and have on-going relationships with those outside the church?

_____

_____

_____

_____

Write a sentence that illustrates the impact daily prayer to God can have upon a Christian woman's *walk* in Christ.

_____

_____

_____

_____

Alphabet of A Praying Christian Woman

X

Xiphoid

*(**NOTE**: Finding no appropriate "X" word in scripture, the word "Xiphoid," which means, "having the shape of a **sword**" was chosen for this exercise.)*

"And taking the helmet of salvation and the *sword* of the Spirit, which is the word of God, and pray in the Spirit on all occasions, with all kinds of prayers and requests. With this in mind, be alert and always keep on praying for all the saints." (Ephesians 6: 17)

In the space below, record other scriptures where God's word is referred to as the *sword*.

_____

_____

_____

_____

The *Hebrews* writer gave a vivid illustration of the power of the *sword* as it represents the word of God. Explain how the power of prayer can produce equivalent results as a *sword* of truth.

_____

_____

_____

_____

In your opinion, is the simile of the word of God
as a *sword* a fitting one? Why or why not?

_____

_____

_____

_____

Alphabet of A Praying Christian Woman

Y

Yoke

"Take My *yoke* upon you and learn of Me, for I am
gentle and lowly in heart," (Matthew 11: 29)

In Paul's letter to the Romans, he explained that "*anyone who
has died has been freed from sin.*" How can a Christian take
on a *yoke* of Christ and still consider them self as free?

_____

_____

_____

_____

In your opinion, what is the *yoke* Christ expects a Christian to bear?

_____

_____

_____

_____

Write a sentence that illustrates the components of
the *yoke* Christ expects a Christian to bear.

_____

_____

_____

_____

Alphabet of A Praying Christian Woman

Z

Zealous

"For it is good to be *zealous* in a good thing always," (Galatians 4: 18)

How is it possible for a Christian woman not to be good toward others while being *zealous* in her prayer life?

_____

_____

_____

_____

In your opinion, can a Christian be over *zealous*
in prayer? Explain you answer.

_____

_____

_____

_____

How would you react to being considered an overly *zealous*
Christian and how would you approach this issue in prayer?

_____

_____

_____

_____

Epilogue
THE CONCEPT OF PRAYER

Holding on to the concept of Christ's ever presence with those who have chosen to follow His teachings should always be a comfort and a source of peace. However, Christians can often become so involved with the issues of this life we are apt to forget for a time the comfort and peace Christ provides. Too often we attempt to carry our burdens on our own.

Following the crucifixion, the disciples were in turmoil as they tried to sort out the events of recent days. They were confused and disoriented concerning what they were to do. When Christ first appeared to them, His first words were, *"Peace be with you."* (Luke 24: 36b). Christ desired the disciples to have peace within themselves.

Looking back at the history that followed the disciples and especially the apostles of Christ during the first century, we realize they suffered much for their dedication and faith in the Savior. They experienced very little peace in their physical lives, as many were persecuted, imprisoned, beaten, stoned, exiled, beheaded, and even crucified. What happened to the "peace" Christ desired for them?

The "peace" Christ offered His disciples is found in the love He held for them, as well as all those who follow His teachings today. Conversely, Christians find "peace" through love for God and Christ Jesus, His Son. Our love for Christ is revealed through our daily relationship with Him – a relationship enhanced and made whole through prayer.

The apostle Paul explained his expression of love for Christ, as well as others, in his first epistle to the Corinthians when he wrote: *"If I give all I possess to the poor and surrender my body to the flames, but have not love, I gain nothing.* (*1 Corinthians 13: 3*). Through the understanding of this verse alone, we can discern Paul's relationship with Christ and know Paul was at *peace.*

The apostle Paul further illustrated this *peace* when he instructed the Philippians: "*Therefore, my dear friends, as you have always obeyed not only in my presence, but now much more in my absence – continue to work out your salvation with fear and trembling, for it is God who works in you to will and to act according to his good purpose. Do everything without complaining or arguing, so that you can become blameless and pure, children of God without fault in a crooked and depraved generation, in which you shine like stars in the universe, as you hold out the word of life – in order that I may boast on the day of Christ that I did not run or labor for nothing.*" (*Philippians 2: 12-16*)

Of course, no one could have given us a better under- standing of the inclusiveness of God's blessings than Christ. In the gospel of Matthew we find the ***Beatitudes***, which exemplify those who are or *will be blessed. Christ used these definitive descriptions for the blessed* to open His Sermon on the Mount.

By incorporating the lessons found in Matthew, Chapters 5 through 7, which constitute the Sermon on the Mount, Christians are given a clear explanation of what is expected of us. A key part of Christ's message included the concept of prayer – as a private matter between the Christian and God the Father; as a matter of attitude, of reverence, and respect; and as a matter of sustaining a lasting relationship with God the Father.

During this portion of His dissertation, Christ offered what has become known as "**The LORD's Prayer:**" Christ lead into His example of prayer with, "*This, then, is how you should pray:*

'*Our Father in heaven, hallowed be Your name, Your kingdom come, Your will be done on earth as it is in heaven. Give us today our daily bread. Forgive us our debts, as we also have forgiven our debtors. And lead us not into temptation, but deliver us from the evil one.*'" (*Matthew 6: 9-13*)

Assimilating the lessons, with their specific ideologies, into our own personalities and our character are essential to being among the blessed. As Christ further explained, *"For if you forgive men when they sin against you, your heavenly Father will also forgive you. But if you do not forgive men their sins, your Father will not forgive your sins. (Matthew 6: 14-15)*

Having followed Jesus for at least three years, the disciples had learned not only to love and trust Him, but to find comfort in His teachings, as well as in His presence. In conveying to His disciples He would be going away to *"prepare a place,"* Christ stated, *"You know the place where I am going."* (*John: 14: 4*). However, Christ found need to give them additional instructions concerning His destiny, due to confusion remaining in their minds, when He explained, *"I am the way and the truth and the life."* (John 14: 6)

To reassure His disciples they would be cared for once He had fulfilled His mission on earth, Christ offered them solace with these words, *"And I will pray to the Father and He shall give you another Comforter, that He may abide with you forever;"* (*John 14: 16*). The Comforter – the Holy Spirit – as promised was given not only for those disciples, but for all those who obey His word. The disciples expected Christ's prayer to the Father for a Comforter to be answered.

When we pray, we must expect our Father to give us comfort through the answers to our prayers. However, we must keep in mind the words of James, *"When you ask, you do not receive, because you ask amiss* (with wrong motives) *that you may spend what you get on your pleasures."* (*James 4: 4*).

There are at least three possible answers God may give to our prayers: "YES," "NO," or "WAIT A WHILE." There may be many times when answer to prayer is not immediately realized – although, the answer has been given. Most likely, it is because the answer was not exactly as we expected it to be given.

Consider a prayer for a friend or loved one who is battling a critical illness – one which the prognosis indicates the condition is terminal. Prayer requests for the individual cover such things as relief from pain, comforting rest, healing, guidance for the doctors treating the patient, etc.

Often a patient in such a critical condition continues to live well beyond the time given in the doctor's prognosis. Although this may occur, as time passes, the patient's health diminishes and they eventually pass away. Looking back on this situation, did God answer the prayers of those who sought relief from pain, comforting rest, healing, and/or guidance for the doctors treating the patient? Did the answer result in a better life for the afflicted one and/or their family? Think reflectively to find the answers to these questions.

Prayer can provide peace to those who seek it as Christ offered it to His disciples at the time He appeared to them following His resurrection. When a Christian desires peace, God will give them the kind of peace they truly need. We must realize just what true peace is and we need also to realize what peace means as we pray to God the Father as though we are a child – His child!